LEADERSHIP LEGACY

Nurturing Authentic Influence and Impactful Management

NANCY BARLOW

Copyright © 2024 by Nancy Barlow

All rights reserved. No part of this book may be reproduced, stored in a retrieval system, or transmitted, in any form or by any means, electronic, mechanical, photocopying, recording, or otherwise, without the prior written permission of the author, except in the case of brief quotations embodied in critical reviews and certain other noncommercial uses permitted by copyright law.

TABLE OF CONTENT

INTRODUCTION 5

CHAPTER 1: THE ESSENCE OF AUTHENTIC LEADERSHIP 7

- Understanding Authenticity in Leadership 8
- Building Trust and Credibility 13
- Balancing Vulnerability and Strength 18

CHAPTER 2: NURTURING MEANINGFUL CONNECTIONS 24

- Cultivating Relationships with Stakeholders .. 25
- Communicating with Transparency and Empathy 32
- Creating a Culture of Collaboration 37

CHAPTER 3: IMPACTFUL MANAGEMENT PRACTICES 45

- Setting Clear Goals and Expectations 46
- Empowering Teams and Individuals 53
- Driving Innovation and Adaptability 60

CHAPTER 4: LEADING THROUGH CHANGE AND CHALLENGES 67

- Embracing Change as a Catalyst for Growth . 68

- Resilience in the Face of Adversity 75

- Strategies for Managing Conflict Effectively . 81

CHAPTER 5: LEAVING A LASTING LEADERSHIP LEGACY 89

- Defining Your Leadership Legacy Vision 90

- Mentoring and Developing Future Leaders 97

- Sustaining a Legacy of Impact and Influence 105

CONCLUSION 112

INTRODUCTION

In the realm of leadership, the echo of one's influence transcends mere authority; it leaves a lasting legacy woven into the fabric of organizational culture. "Leadership Legacy: Nurturing Authentic Influence and Impactful Management" delves into the heart of leadership, where authenticity and impactful management converge to shape a legacy that endures.

In this insightful guide, we explore the essence of authentic leadership and the profound impact it has on individuals, teams, and organizations. Through practical strategies and real-world examples, we navigate the complexities of leadership, emphasizing the importance of nurturing genuine connections, fostering trust, and driving positive change.

Drawing on decades of collective wisdom and experience, this book offers a roadmap for aspiring leaders, seasoned executives, and anyone passionate about making a difference. Whether you're leading a small team or steering a large organization, the principles outlined here empower you to cultivate a leadership legacy that inspires, influences, and leaves a meaningful imprint on those you lead.

Join us on a journey of discovery, where leadership transcends titles and transforms into a legacy of enduring impact. It's time to unleash your authentic influence and embark on a path of transformative leadership that leaves a lasting legacy for generations to come.

CHAPTER 1: THE ESSENCE OF AUTHENTIC LEADERSHIP

In the dynamic landscape of leadership, authenticity serves as the bedrock upon which impactful influence is built. This chapter delves into the core principles of authentic leadership, illuminating the path for leaders to discover their true selves and lead with integrity and purpose.

Authentic leadership goes beyond mere actions and decisions; it embodies a genuine alignment between values, beliefs, and actions. As we embark on this exploration, we uncover the essence of what it means to lead authentically, forging connections based on trust, transparency, and empathy.

Join us in unraveling the intricacies of authentic leadership, as we delve into the key components that define this transformative approach to leading with authenticity and influence.

- Understanding Authenticity in Leadership

Authenticity in leadership is a foundational concept that underpins effective and sustainable leadership practices. It refers to the alignment between a leader's values, beliefs, and actions, creating a sense of genuineness and transparency in their leadership style. In this discussion, we'll comprehensively explore what authenticity means in the context of leadership, why it's important, how it can be cultivated, and its impact on individuals, teams, and organizations.

Definition and Components of Authentic Leadership

Authentic leadership is often described as being true to oneself while leading others. It involves being aware of one's values, strengths, weaknesses, and motivations, and integrating these aspects into leadership practices. Key components of authentic leadership include:

1. **Self-Awareness:** Authentic leaders have a deep understanding of their strengths, weaknesses, values, and emotions. They are self-reflective and continually strive to align their actions with their core beliefs.

2. **Transparency:** Authentic leaders are open and honest in their communication. They share information openly, admit mistakes, and seek feedback from others, fostering trust and credibility.

3. **Consistency:** Authentic leaders demonstrate consistency in their words and actions. They do not waver from their values and principles, even in challenging situations.

4. **Empathy:** Authentic leaders show empathy and compassion towards others. They listen actively,

understand different perspectives, and consider the impact of their decisions on individuals and teams.

Importance of Authentic Leadership

Authentic leadership is crucial for several reasons:

1. **Building Trust:** Authentic leaders build trust and credibility among their team members and stakeholders. When leaders are authentic, employees feel more comfortable sharing ideas, raising concerns, and engaging in open dialogue.

2. **Enhancing Employee Engagement:** Authentic leaders inspire and motivate their teams by demonstrating genuine passion and commitment. This leads to higher levels of employee engagement, productivity, and job satisfaction.

3. **Driving Organizational Culture:** Authentic leaders play a significant role in shaping organizational culture. By embodying values such as integrity, honesty, and transparency, they create a positive work environment where values alignment is prioritized.

4. **Fostering Innovation:** Authentic leaders encourage creativity and innovation by creating a safe space for experimentation and risk-taking. They value diverse perspectives and empower employees to contribute their ideas and insights.

Cultivating Authentic Leadership

Authentic leadership can be cultivated through various strategies:

1. **Self-Reflection:** Leaders can enhance their authenticity by engaging in regular self-reflection and introspection. This involves exploring personal values, strengths, weaknesses, and areas for growth.

2. **Seeking Feedback:** Leaders should actively seek feedback from peers, mentors, and team members to gain insights into how their behavior is perceived and how they can improve their authenticity.

3. **Building Relationships:** Authentic leaders prioritize building meaningful relationships based on trust, respect, and empathy. They invest time in getting to know their team members as individuals and understanding their needs and aspirations.

4. **Leading by Example:** Authentic leaders lead by example, demonstrating integrity, transparency, and consistency in their actions. They uphold ethical standards and hold themselves accountable for their decisions and behaviors.

Impact of Authentic Leadership

The impact of authentic leadership is far-reaching:

1. **Employee Engagement:** Authentic leaders foster a sense of purpose and belonging among employees, leading to higher levels of engagement, commitment, and loyalty.

2. **Organizational Performance:** Authentic leadership contributes to improved organizational performance, as employees are motivated to achieve goals and contribute their best efforts.

3. **Innovation and Creativity:** Authentic leaders encourage innovation and creativity by creating an environment where diverse ideas are welcomed and valued.

4. **Employee Well-Being:** Authentic leaders prioritize employee well-being and mental health, creating a supportive work culture that promotes work-life balance and reduces stress.

In conclusion, understanding authenticity in leadership is fundamental to creating positive and impactful leadership experiences. By cultivating authenticity, leaders can build trust, inspire others, drive organizational success, and leave a lasting legacy of positive influence and impact.

- Building Trust and Credibility

Building trust and credibility is a cornerstone of effective leadership. It forms the foundation of strong relationships between leaders and their teams, fosters collaboration, enhances communication, and drives organizational success. In this comprehensive discussion, we will explore the importance of trust and credibility in leadership, strategies for building and maintaining them, and their impact on individuals, teams, and organizations.

Importance of Trust and Credibility

Trust and credibility are vital for several reasons:

1. **Team Cohesion:** Trust fosters a sense of unity and cohesion within teams. When team members trust their leaders, they are more likely to collaborate effectively, share ideas openly, and work towards common goals.

2. **Employee Engagement:** Trust and credibility contribute to higher levels of employee engagement. When employees trust their leaders, they are more engaged, motivated, and committed to achieving organizational objectives.

3. **Effective Communication:** Trust enhances communication by creating an environment where open and honest dialogue is encouraged. Leaders who are trusted are more likely to receive candid feedback, address concerns proactively, and resolve conflicts constructively.

4. **Organizational Reputation:** Trust and credibility are key components of an organization's reputation. Leaders who are trusted by their employees, customers, and stakeholders enhance the organization's image and brand reputation.

Strategies for Building Trust and Credibility

Building trust and credibility is an ongoing process that requires intentional effort and consistent actions. Some strategies to consider include:

1. **Lead with Integrity:** Integrity is fundamental to building trust and credibility. Leaders should demonstrate honesty, transparency, and ethical behavior in all their interactions.

2. **Communicate Effectively:** Clear and open communication is essential for building trust. Leaders should communicate openly, listen actively, and provide regular updates and feedback to their teams.

3. **Demonstrate Competence:** Leaders should demonstrate competence and expertise in their roles. By showcasing knowledge, skills, and

experience, they earn the trust and respect of their teams.

4. **Be Consistent:** Consistency in words and actions is key to building trust. Leaders should follow through on commitments, adhere to values and principles, and avoid contradictory behavior.

5. **Empower and Delegate:** Trusting team members with responsibilities and empowering them to make decisions builds trust and confidence. Leaders should delegate effectively, provide support and guidance, and recognize and reward achievements.

6. **Admit Mistakes and Learn:** Leaders should be willing to admit mistakes, take responsibility, and learn from failures. Acknowledging vulnerabilities and demonstrating resilience builds trust and credibility.

Impact of Trust and Credibility

The impact of trust and credibility in leadership is profound:

1. **Employee Loyalty:** Trusted leaders inspire loyalty and commitment among employees. When employees trust their leaders, they are more likely to stay with the organization, contribute their best efforts, and advocate for the organization.

2. **Conflict Resolution:** Trust facilitates effective conflict resolution. When trust exists between leaders and team members, conflicts are addressed openly and resolved collaboratively, without damaging relationships.

3. **Innovation and Risk-Taking**: Trust encourages innovation and risk-taking. Employees feel empowered to explore new ideas, take calculated risks, and contribute to continuous improvement when they trust their leaders' support and guidance.

4. **Organizational Resilience:** Trust and credibility contribute to organizational resilience. In times of change, challenge, or crisis, trusted leaders can navigate uncertainty, inspire confidence, and lead teams through adversity.

In conclusion, building trust and credibility is a fundamental aspect of effective leadership. Leaders who prioritize trust and credibility create environments where individuals thrive, teams collaborate effectively, and organizations achieve sustainable success. By investing in building and maintaining trust, leaders lay the groundwork for enduring relationships, enhanced performance, and a positive organizational culture.

- Balancing Vulnerability and Strength

Balancing vulnerability and strength is a nuanced aspect of leadership that involves navigating the delicate balance between openness and resilience. In this comprehensive discussion, we will explore what vulnerability and strength mean in the context of leadership, why finding this balance is important, strategies for achieving it, and the impact it has on leaders, teams, and organizations.

Understanding Vulnerability and Strength in Leadership

Vulnerability in leadership refers to the willingness to be open, authentic, and transparent about one's thoughts, feelings, and challenges. It involves admitting mistakes, asking for help, and showing empathy towards others. Strength, on the other hand, encompasses resilience, determination, and the ability to lead with confidence and conviction.

Importance of Balancing Vulnerability and Strength

Balancing vulnerability and strength is crucial for several reasons:

1. **Building Trust:** Vulnerability can foster trust by demonstrating authenticity and humility. However, strength is also necessary to inspire confidence and provide direction.

2. **Encouraging Growth:** Embracing vulnerability allows leaders to learn from failures and setbacks, fostering personal and professional growth. Strength

enables leaders to persevere and lead with resilience.

3. **Fostering Innovation:** Vulnerability encourages creativity and innovation by creating a safe space for experimentation and risk-taking. Strength ensures that ideas are implemented effectively and goals are achieved.

4. **Enhancing Relationships**: Balancing vulnerability and strength leads to deeper and more meaningful relationships with team members, as it allows for open communication, trust, and empathy.

Strategies for Balancing Vulnerability and Strength

Achieving a balance between vulnerability and strength requires intentional effort and self-awareness. Some strategies to consider include:

1. **Know Yourself:** Leaders should have a deep understanding of their strengths, weaknesses, values, and emotions. This self-awareness enables them to navigate vulnerabilities while leveraging their strengths.

2. **Practice Authenticity:** Authenticity involves being true to oneself and others. Leaders should be open and transparent about their thoughts, feelings, and challenges, while also demonstrating confidence and resilience.

3. **Seek Feedback:** Leaders should actively seek feedback from peers, mentors, and team members to gain insights into how their vulnerability and strength are perceived and how they can improve their leadership approach.

4. **Embrace Learning:** Vulnerability involves admitting mistakes and being open to learning and growth. Leaders should view failures as opportunities for improvement and encourage a culture of continuous learning within their teams.

5. **Lead with Empathy:** Empathy is a powerful tool for balancing vulnerability and strength. Leaders should show empathy towards others, listen actively, and consider the impact of their actions on individuals and teams.

Impact of Balancing Vulnerability and Strength

The impact of balancing vulnerability and strength is profound:

1. **Trust and Respect:** Balancing vulnerability and strength builds trust and respect among team members. When leaders are authentic and open, they inspire trust and confidence, leading to stronger relationships and collaboration.

2. **Resilience and Adaptability**: Balancing vulnerability and strength enhances resilience and adaptability. Leaders who embrace vulnerability learn from challenges and setbacks, while strength enables them to navigate change and uncertainty effectively.

3. **Employee Engagement:** Balancing vulnerability and strength contributes to higher levels of employee engagement. When leaders show vulnerability, employees feel valued, heard, and motivated to contribute their best efforts.

4. **Innovation and Creativity:** Balancing vulnerability and strength fosters a culture of innovation and creativity. Leaders who encourage risk-taking and experimentation while providing guidance and support inspire innovation within their teams.

In conclusion, balancing vulnerability and strength is a dynamic process that requires self-awareness, authenticity, and empathy. Leaders who find this balance create environments where trust, resilience, and innovation thrive, leading to enhanced performance and a positive organizational culture. By embracing vulnerability and leveraging strength, leaders can inspire and empower their teams to achieve extraordinary results.

CHAPTER 2: NURTURING MEANINGFUL CONNECTIONS

In the realm of leadership, the ability to foster meaningful connections lies at the heart of building strong and cohesive teams. Chapter 2 delves into the art of nurturing these connections, exploring the dynamics of relationships within organizations and the profound impact they have on individual growth and collective success.

Meaningful connections go beyond mere interactions; they are built on a foundation of trust, respect, and empathy. As we embark on this journey, we unravel the strategies and principles that leaders can employ to cultivate authentic relationships, foster collaboration, and create a sense of belonging within their teams.

Join us in exploring the transformative power of meaningful connections, where every interaction becomes an opportunity for growth, understanding, and shared purpose. It's time to unlock the potential of human connections and harness their immense influence in shaping a thriving organizational culture.

- Cultivating Relationships with Stakeholders

In the landscape of leadership and organizational management, cultivating strong relationships with stakeholders is essential for sustained success and growth. Stakeholders encompass a wide range of individuals and groups, including employees, customers, investors, partners, regulators, and the community at large. In this comprehensive discussion, we will delve into the importance of cultivating relationships with stakeholders, strategies for effective stakeholder management, challenges to consider, and the impact of strong stakeholder relationships on organizational outcomes.

Importance of Cultivating Relationships with Stakeholders

1. **Building Trust and Credibility:** Strong relationships with stakeholders build trust and credibility, which are fundamental to achieving organizational goals, securing investments, and fostering a positive reputation.

2. **Understanding Needs and Expectations:** Cultivating relationships with stakeholders allows leaders to gain insights into their needs, expectations, and concerns. This understanding enables organizations to tailor their strategies, products, and services to meet stakeholder requirements effectively.

3. **Creating Synergies and Partnerships:** Collaborative relationships with stakeholders create opportunities for synergies, partnerships, and strategic alliances. These partnerships can lead to

innovation, market expansion, and mutual benefits for all parties involved.

4. **Managing Risks and Resolving Conflicts:** Strong stakeholder relationships facilitate effective risk management and conflict resolution. Open communication and trust enable organizations to address issues proactively, minimize disruptions, and maintain stability.

Strategies for Effective Stakeholder Management

1. **Identify Key Stakeholders:** Begin by identifying key stakeholders who have a significant impact on or are impacted by the organization's activities, decisions, and outcomes. This includes internal stakeholders (employees, management) and external stakeholders (customers, investors, regulators, community).

2. **Engage in Dialogue:** Foster open and ongoing dialogue with stakeholders to understand their perspectives, concerns, and expectations. This can be achieved through meetings, surveys, focus

groups, town hall sessions, and regular communication channels.

3. **Listen Actively:** Actively listen to stakeholder feedback, suggestions, and criticisms. Demonstrate empathy, respect, and a willingness to address their needs and concerns.

4. **Transparent Communication:** Practice transparent and honest communication with stakeholders, sharing relevant information about the organization's goals, strategies, performance, and challenges. Transparency builds trust and credibility.

5. **Set Mutual Goals:** Collaborate with stakeholders to set mutual goals and objectives aligned with the organization's mission and values. Engage stakeholders in decision-making processes that impact them directly.

6. **Provide Value:** Demonstrate the value proposition of engaging with the organization by delivering quality products, services, and

experiences that meet stakeholder expectations and contribute to their success.

7. Build Relationships Over Time: Cultivating relationships with stakeholders is a long-term endeavor. Invest time and effort in building rapport, maintaining regular contact, and nurturing trust-based relationships.

Challenges in Stakeholder Management

1. **Diverse Stakeholder Interests:** Stakeholders often have diverse and sometimes conflicting interests, priorities, and agendas. Balancing these interests while meeting organizational objectives can be challenging.

2. **Managing Expectations:** Stakeholders may have high expectations regarding performance, results, and outcomes. Managing these expectations effectively requires clear communication, realistic goal-setting, and transparency.

3. **Changing Stakeholder Dynamics:** Stakeholder relationships can evolve over time due to changes in leadership, market conditions, regulations, or

stakeholder priorities. Organizations must adapt and navigate these changing dynamics.

4. Resolving Conflicts: Conflicts may arise between stakeholders or between stakeholders and the organization. Effective conflict resolution strategies, such as mediation, negotiation, and compromise, are essential for maintaining positive relationships.

Impact of Strong Stakeholder Relationships

1. **Enhanced Reputation:** Strong stakeholder relationships contribute to a positive organizational reputation, which can attract customers, investors, and talent.

2. **Innovation and Collaboration:** Collaborative relationships with stakeholders foster innovation, knowledge sharing, and collaboration, leading to new opportunities and competitive advantages.

3. **Risk Mitigation:** Proactively managing stakeholder relationships helps mitigate risks, such as reputational risks, regulatory risks, and

operational risks, by addressing issues early and maintaining trust.

4. Sustainability and Social Responsibility: Engaging with stakeholders on sustainability and social responsibility initiatives builds credibility, trust, and loyalty while contributing to positive societal impact.

In conclusion, cultivating relationships with stakeholders is a strategic imperative for organizations seeking sustained success, growth, and impact. By prioritizing open communication, trust-building, collaboration, and mutual value creation, leaders can strengthen stakeholder relationships, navigate challenges effectively, and achieve shared goals and outcomes.

Communicating with Transparency and Empathy

Effective communication is the cornerstone of successful leadership, and when combined with transparency and empathy, it becomes a powerful tool for building trust, fostering collaboration, and creating a positive organizational culture. In this comprehensive discussion, we will delve into the importance of communicating with transparency and empathy, strategies for doing so effectively, the impact it has on stakeholders, and how it contributes to overall leadership effectiveness.

Importance of Communicating with Transparency and Empathy

1. Building Trust: Transparent and empathetic communication builds trust among stakeholders, including employees, customers, investors, and partners. When people feel that information is shared openly and honestly, they are more likely to trust leaders and the organization as a whole.

2. **Enhancing Engagement:** Transparent and empathetic communication enhances engagement by making individuals feel valued, heard, and understood. When leaders communicate with empathy, they show genuine concern for the well-being and perspectives of others, leading to increased motivation and commitment.

3. **Creating Clarity:** Transparent communication provides clarity and reduces ambiguity. When expectations, goals, and decisions are communicated clearly and openly, it reduces confusion, misunderstandings, and conflicts within the organization.

4. **Fostering Collaboration:** Empathetic communication fosters collaboration by promoting understanding, respect, and mutual support among team members. When individuals feel that their opinions and feelings are acknowledged and

respected, they are more likely to collaborate effectively towards common goals.

Strategies for Communicating with Transparency and Empathy

1. **Be Honest and Open:** Communicate information honestly and openly, avoiding misleading or deceptive statements. Share both good news and challenges transparently, providing context and explanations where necessary.

2. **Listen Actively**: Practice active listening by paying attention to others' perspectives, feelings, and concerns. Show empathy by acknowledging emotions, validating experiences, and demonstrating understanding.

3. **Use Clear and Simple Language**: Use clear, simple, and jargon-free language when communicating complex information. Avoid ambiguity and ensure that messages are easily understood by all stakeholders.

4. **Provide Context and Rationale:** When sharing decisions or changes, provide context and rationale to help stakeholders understand the reasoning behind them. This helps build trust and reduces resistance or confusion.

5. **Seek Feedback:** Encourage feedback from stakeholders and be open to receiving constructive criticism. Act on feedback by addressing concerns, making improvements, and communicating outcomes.

6. **Be Responsive:** Respond promptly to inquiries, requests, and concerns from stakeholders. Demonstrate that their input is valued and that their voices are heard.

7. **Show Empathy:** Demonstrate empathy by considering others' perspectives, feelings, and needs. Acknowledge emotions, show understanding, and respond with compassion and support.

Impact of Communicating with Transparency and Empathy

1. **Trust and Credibility:** Transparent and empathetic communication builds trust and credibility among stakeholders, leading to stronger relationships and increased loyalty.

2. **Employee Engagement:** Transparent and empathetic communication enhances employee engagement, motivation, and job satisfaction. Employees feel valued, heard, and connected to the organization's goals and values.

3. **Conflict Resolution:** Transparent and empathetic communication facilitates effective conflict resolution by promoting understanding, empathy, and collaborative problem-solving.

4. **Innovation and Collaboration:** Transparent and empathetic communication fosters innovation and collaboration by creating an environment where diverse perspectives are valued, ideas are shared openly, and collaboration is encouraged.

5. **Organizational Culture:** Transparent and empathetic communication contributes to a positive organizational culture characterized by trust,

openness, and mutual respect. This culture attracts talent, fosters creativity, and supports organizational resilience.

In conclusion, communicating with transparency and empathy is a fundamental aspect of effective leadership. By prioritizing open, honest, and empathetic communication, leaders can build trust, enhance engagement, foster collaboration, and create a culture of transparency and accountability within their organizations. Transparent and empathetic communication not only strengthens relationships with stakeholders but also drives organizational success and sustainability in the long term.

- Creating a Culture of Collaboration

A culture of collaboration is a fundamental element of high-performing organizations, driving innovation, productivity, and engagement among employees. In this comprehensive discussion, we will explore what a culture of collaboration entails, why it is important, strategies for creating and nurturing such a culture, challenges to consider, and the impact it has on organizational success.

Definition of a Culture of Collaboration

A culture of collaboration refers to an environment where teamwork, communication, and cooperation are valued and encouraged. It involves breaking down silos, fostering open dialogue, sharing knowledge and resources, and working towards common goals across teams and departments.

Importance of Creating a Culture of Collaboration

1. **Innovation:** Collaboration stimulates creativity and innovation by bringing together diverse perspectives, ideas, and expertise. It leads to new insights, solutions, and opportunities for growth and development.

2. **Productivity:** Collaboration enhances productivity by streamlining processes, reducing duplication of efforts, and leveraging collective strengths. Teams that collaborate effectively can achieve more in less time and with fewer resources.

3. **Engagement:** A culture of collaboration increases employee engagement by fostering a sense of belonging, purpose, and contribution. When employees collaborate and see the impact of their work, they feel motivated and invested in the organization's success.

4. **Learning and Development:** Collaboration promotes continuous learning and development by encouraging knowledge sharing, skill-building, and cross-functional experiences. It creates a culture of learning where individuals and teams are empowered to grow and adapt.

Strategies for Creating a Culture of Collaboration

1. **Leadership Commitment:** Leadership plays a crucial role in creating a culture of collaboration.

Leaders should demonstrate and promote collaboration through their actions, decisions, and communication. They should set the tone for collaboration and encourage participation from all levels of the organization.

2. Clear Goals and Objectives: Establish clear goals, objectives, and priorities that align with the organization's mission and values. Communicate these goals transparently and ensure that teams understand how their work contributes to broader organizational objectives.

3. Open Communication: Foster open and transparent communication channels across teams and departments. Encourage feedback, ideas, and suggestions from employees, and provide opportunities for dialogue and discussion.

4. Cross-Functional Teams: Create cross-functional teams that bring together individuals from different backgrounds, expertise areas, and perspectives. Encourage collaboration and knowledge sharing within these teams to drive innovation and problem-solving.

5. **Technology and Tools:** Invest in collaboration tools and technology that facilitate communication, document sharing, project management, and virtual collaboration. Ensure that employees have access to the tools they need to collaborate effectively, whether they are working remotely or in-office.

6. **Recognition and Rewards:** Recognize and reward collaborative behaviors and achievements. Celebrate teamwork, collaboration success stories, and contributions that demonstrate a commitment to collaboration and shared goals.

7. **Training and Development:** Provide training and development opportunities that promote collaboration skills, such as teamwork, communication, conflict resolution, and decision-making. Encourage continuous learning and improvement in collaboration practices.

Challenges in Creating a Culture of Collaboration

1. **Silos and Departmental Barriers:** Overcoming silos and departmental barriers can be a challenge in creating a culture of collaboration. Leaders must promote cross-functional collaboration and break down barriers that hinder communication and cooperation.

2. **Resistance to Change:** Some employees may resist changes to traditional ways of working or collaborating. Leaders should communicate the benefits of collaboration, address concerns, and involve employees in the process of creating a collaborative culture.

3. **Communication Breakdowns:** Miscommunication, lack of clarity, and misunderstandings can impede collaboration. Leaders should ensure that communication channels are effective, information is shared transparently, and expectations are clear.

4. **Workload and Prioritization:** Balancing collaboration with individual workloads and priorities can be challenging. Leaders should help

teams prioritize tasks, manage workloads effectively, and allocate resources strategically to support collaboration efforts.

Impact of a Culture of Collaboration

1. **Innovation and Creativity:** A culture of collaboration fosters innovation and creativity by encouraging diverse perspectives, idea sharing, and experimentation. It leads to new solutions, products, and services that drive organizational growth and competitiveness.

2. **Employee Engagement and Satisfaction:** Collaboration increases employee engagement and satisfaction by creating a sense of belonging, ownership, and purpose. Employees feel valued, supported, and motivated to contribute their best efforts.

3. **Efficiency and Effectiveness:** Collaborative teams are more efficient and effective in achieving goals and delivering results. They leverage collective strengths, resources, and expertise to

solve problems, make decisions, and drive outcomes.

4. **Organizational Resilience:** Collaboration enhances organizational resilience by building strong relationships, trust, and communication channels. In times of change, challenge, or crisis, collaborative cultures adapt quickly, innovate solutions, and navigate complexities effectively.

In conclusion, creating a culture of collaboration is a strategic imperative for organizations seeking sustained success, innovation, and competitive advantage. By fostering open communication, teamwork, and shared goals, leaders can cultivate a collaborative culture that empowers employees, drives performance, and fuels organizational growth and resilience. Collaborative cultures not only benefit individuals and teams but also contribute to a positive work environment, organizational reputation, and long-term success.

CHAPTER 3: IMPACTFUL MANAGEMENT PRACTICES

Effective management is the cornerstone of organizational success, guiding teams towards achieving goals, fostering innovation, and driving growth. Chapter 3 delves into the realm of impactful management practices, exploring strategies, principles, and approaches that leaders can leverage to inspire excellence, maximize performance, and create a culture of success within their teams and organizations.

In this chapter, we embark on a journey to uncover the essential elements of impactful management, from setting clear goals and expectations to empowering teams, driving innovation, and adapting to change. Through practical insights, real-world examples, and actionable techniques, we explore how effective management practices can transform challenges into opportunities and propel organizations towards sustainable success.

Join us as we navigate the dynamic landscape of management, where leadership meets execution, and every decision, action, and interaction shapes the path to achieving strategic objectives and leaving a lasting impact on individuals, teams, and the broader organizational ecosystem. It's time to unlock the potential of impactful management practices and unleash the full potential of your leadership capabilities.

- Setting Clear Goals and Expectations

Setting clear goals and expectations is a foundational aspect of effective management and leadership. It provides direction, clarity, and alignment within teams and organizations, guiding efforts towards achieving desired outcomes. In this comprehensive discussion, we will explore the importance of setting clear goals and expectations, strategies for doing so effectively, challenges to consider, and the impact it has on organizational performance and employee engagement.

Importance of Setting Clear Goals and Expectations

1. **Alignment:** Clear goals and expectations align individuals and teams with the organization's mission, vision, and strategic objectives. They provide a roadmap for decision-making, resource allocation, and prioritization of tasks and projects.

2. **Focus and Prioritization:** Clear goals and expectations help teams focus on key priorities and tasks, reducing distractions and unnecessary efforts. They enable teams to allocate resources efficiently and achieve results effectively.

3. **Motivation and Engagement:** Defined goals and expectations motivate and engage employees by providing a sense of purpose, direction, and achievement. They create a framework for

performance measurement, feedback, and recognition.

4. **Accountability:** Clear goals and expectations foster accountability and responsibility among team members. They establish standards of performance, milestones, and deadlines, helping teams track progress and take ownership of outcomes.

Strategies for Setting Clear Goals and Expectations

1. **SMART Goals:** Use the SMART framework (Specific, Measurable, Achievable, Relevant, Time-bound) to set clear and actionable goals. Ensure that goals are specific, quantifiable, realistic, aligned with the organization's objectives, and have defined timelines for completion.

2. **Communicate Effectively:** Communicate goals and expectations clearly and consistently to all stakeholders, including team members, supervisors, and partners. Use multiple communication channels, such as meetings, emails, and

presentations, to ensure understanding and alignment.

3. **Collaborative Goal-Setting:** Involve team members in the goal-setting process to gain buy-in, foster engagement, and promote ownership. Encourage input, feedback, and ideas for setting realistic and achievable goals.

4. **Provide Clarity:** Clarify roles, responsibilities, and performance expectations associated with each goal. Define key performance indicators (KPIs), success criteria, and milestones to track progress and evaluate performance.

5. **Set Priorities:** Prioritize goals based on importance, urgency, and impact on organizational objectives. Ensure that resources, time, and effort are allocated effectively to high-priority goals that contribute significantly to strategic outcomes.

6. **Regular Monitoring and Review:** Monitor progress towards goals regularly and conduct performance reviews to assess achievements, identify challenges, and make necessary

adjustments. Provide feedback, guidance, and support to help teams stay on track and overcome obstacles.

Challenges in Setting Clear Goals and Expectations

1. **Ambiguity:** Ambiguous or vague goals can lead to confusion, misinterpretation, and lack of clarity among team members. It is essential to articulate goals clearly and provide context, examples, and explanations where necessary.

2. **Changing Priorities:** Shifting priorities or unclear direction from leadership can disrupt goal-setting and implementation. Regular communication, alignment sessions, and flexibility in adapting to changes can mitigate this challenge.

3. **Overloading Goals:** Setting too many goals or unrealistic expectations can overwhelm teams and lead to burnout, stress, and decreased morale. Prioritize goals, set realistic timelines, and ensure that resources are sufficient to support goal achievement.

4. **Lack of Feedback:** Inadequate feedback and performance evaluation can hinder progress towards goals. Establish a feedback loop, provide regular updates, and celebrate milestones to keep teams motivated and informed.

Impact of Setting Clear Goals and Expectations

1. **Improved Performance:** Clear goals and expectations drive improved performance by providing focus, direction, and accountability. Teams are more motivated, engaged, and committed to achieving results when goals are clearly defined and understood.

2. **Enhanced Communication:** Setting clear goals and expectations fosters open communication, transparency, and collaboration within teams. It promotes a shared understanding of objectives, roles, and responsibilities, leading to better coordination and teamwork.

3. **Increased Employee Engagement:** Clear goals and expectations increase employee engagement by providing a sense of purpose, autonomy, and

achievement. Employees feel valued, motivated, and invested in contributing to organizational success.

4. **Efficient Resource Allocation:** Clear goals and expectations help organizations allocate resources efficiently and effectively. Resources such as time, budget, and manpower are aligned with strategic priorities, maximizing their impact and value.

5. **Alignment with Strategic Objectives:** Clear goals and expectations ensure alignment with the organization's strategic objectives, mission, and vision. They guide decision-making, resource allocation, and performance evaluation towards achieving long-term success.

In conclusion, setting clear goals and expectations is a critical aspect of effective management and leadership. By adopting strategies such as SMART goal-setting, effective communication, collaborative engagement, and regular monitoring, organizations can enhance performance, engagement, and alignment with strategic objectives. Clear goals and expectations empower teams to focus on key priorities, drive results, and contribute meaningfully to organizational success.

- Empowering Teams and Individuals

Empowering teams and individuals is a transformative approach to leadership that involves delegating authority, fostering autonomy, and creating an environment where people are empowered to make decisions, take initiative, and contribute their unique skills and perspectives. In this comprehensive discussion, we will explore the importance of empowering teams and individuals, strategies for doing so effectively, challenges to consider, and the impact it has on organizational success and employee engagement.

Importance of Empowering Teams and Individuals

1. **Increased Motivation:** Empowered teams and individuals are more motivated, engaged, and

committed to achieving goals. When people have a sense of ownership and responsibility, they are inspired to perform at their best and take pride in their work.

2. **Enhanced Innovation:** Empowerment fosters a culture of innovation by encouraging creativity, risk-taking, and experimentation. When individuals have the freedom to explore new ideas and solutions, they can contribute to continuous improvement and innovation within the organization.

3. **Improved Decision-Making:** Empowered teams and individuals are equipped to make informed decisions and take appropriate actions. Decentralized decision-making promotes agility, responsiveness, and adaptability in addressing challenges and opportunities.

4. **Skill Development:** Empowerment enables individuals to develop and enhance their skills, knowledge, and capabilities. By taking on new

responsibilities and challenges, they gain valuable experience, confidence, and expertise.

Strategies for Empowering Teams and Individuals

1. **Clarify Roles and Responsibilities:** Clearly define roles, responsibilities, and expectations for team members and individuals. Ensure that everyone understands their areas of authority, decision-making boundaries, and accountability.

2. **Provide Training and Development:** Offer training, mentoring, and coaching to support skill development and capacity-building. Provide opportunities for learning and growth that align with individual aspirations and organizational needs.

3. **Delegate Authority:** Delegate authority and decision-making power to team members based on their capabilities, experience, and expertise. Trust individuals to make decisions and take ownership of their work.

4. **Encourage Autonomy:** Foster autonomy by giving individuals the freedom to choose how they approach tasks, solve problems, and achieve goals. Avoid micromanagement and empower people to work independently and creatively.

5. **Promote Open Communication:** Create a culture of open communication where ideas, feedback, and concerns are welcomed and valued. Encourage dialogue, collaboration, and knowledge sharing among team members and across departments.

6. **Recognize and Reward:** Recognize and reward achievements, contributions, and initiative-taking. Acknowledge and celebrate individual and team successes to reinforce a culture of empowerment and appreciation.

7. **Provide Resources and Support:** Ensure that teams and individuals have access to resources, tools, and support needed to succeed. Address barriers, challenges, and obstacles proactively to enable effective performance and decision-making.

Challenges in Empowering Teams and Individuals

1. **Resistance to Change:** Some individuals may resist empowerment due to fear of failure, lack of confidence, or uncertainty about new responsibilities. Address resistance through communication, support, and training.

2. **Lack of Trust:** Empowerment requires trust between leaders and team members. Build trust through transparency, consistency, and demonstrating confidence in individuals' abilities to take on challenges.

3. **Overcoming Micromanagement:** Leaders may struggle to transition from micromanagement to empowerment. Encourage leaders to let go of control, delegate effectively, and focus on coaching and mentoring rather than direct oversight.

4. **Balancing Autonomy and Accountability:** Empowerment requires striking a balance between autonomy and accountability. Provide autonomy

while also setting clear expectations, performance standards, and feedback mechanisms.

Impact of Empowering Teams and Individuals

1. **Increased Engagement:** Empowered teams and individuals are more engaged, motivated, and committed to achieving goals and driving results. They take ownership of their work, contribute actively, and demonstrate initiative.

2. **Enhanced Innovation and Creativity:** Empowerment fosters a culture of innovation and creativity by encouraging diverse perspectives, idea generation, and experimentation. Teams and individuals feel empowered to explore new ideas, take calculated risks, and innovate solutions.

3. **Improved Decision-Making:** Empowered teams and individuals make better decisions based on their knowledge, expertise, and understanding of the context. Decentralized decision-making leads to faster responses, adaptability, and agility in addressing challenges and opportunities.

4. **Higher Productivity:** Empowered teams and individuals are more productive and efficient in accomplishing tasks and achieving goals. They take initiative, manage their time effectively, and focus on high-impact activities that drive results.

5. **Enhanced Employee Satisfaction:** Empowerment contributes to higher levels of employee satisfaction and morale. Individuals feel valued, trusted, and supported, leading to a positive work environment and stronger employee retention.

In conclusion, empowering teams and individuals is a strategic approach that drives organizational performance, innovation, and employee engagement. By clarifying roles, providing support, fostering autonomy, and promoting open communication, leaders can create a culture of empowerment where individuals thrive, teams collaborate effectively, and organizations achieve sustainable success. Empowerment is not only a leadership strategy but also a mindset that values and leverages the potential of every team member to contribute meaningfully to organizational goals and objectives.

- Driving Innovation and Adaptability

Driving innovation and adaptability is crucial for organizations to stay competitive, respond to market changes, and capitalize on new opportunities. In this comprehensive discussion, we will explore the importance of driving innovation and adaptability, strategies for fostering a culture of innovation, challenges to consider, and the impact it has on organizational success.

Importance of Driving Innovation and Adaptability

1. **Competitive Advantage:** Innovation and adaptability give organizations a competitive edge by enabling them to develop new products, services, and processes that meet evolving customer needs and market trends.

2. **Market Resilience:** Innovation and adaptability help organizations anticipate and respond effectively to changes in the market, industry disruptions, and competitive challenges. They enable organizations to stay agile and resilient in dynamic environments.

3. **Business Growth:** Innovation drives business growth by opening new revenue streams, expanding market reach, and attracting customers with innovative solutions. Adaptability allows organizations to pivot, iterate, and evolve their strategies based on market feedback and insights.

4. **Employee Engagement:** Driving innovation and adaptability engages employees by encouraging creativity, problem-solving, and continuous learning. Employees feel empowered to contribute ideas, experiment with new approaches, and take ownership of driving change within the organization.

Strategies for Driving Innovation and Adaptability

1. **Foster a Culture of Innovation:** Create a culture that values and rewards innovation, creativity, and risk-taking. Encourage curiosity, experimentation, and collaboration among teams and individuals.

2. **Empower Employees:** Empower employees at all levels to contribute ideas, take initiative, and drive innovation. Provide training, resources, and support to help employees develop innovation skills and mindset.

3. **Encourage Cross-Functional Collaboration:** Foster collaboration across departments, teams, and disciplines to leverage diverse perspectives, expertise, and experiences. Cross-functional teams can drive innovation by combining different skill sets and knowledge areas.

4. **Embrace Technology:** Embrace technology and digital tools that enable innovation, automation, and efficiency. Invest in emerging technologies, such as AI, IoT, and data analytics, to drive innovation in

product development, customer experience, and operational excellence.

5. **Customer-Centric Approach:** Adopt a customer-centric approach to innovation by understanding customer needs, preferences, and pain points. Use customer feedback, market research, and design thinking principles to co-create solutions that address customer challenges and deliver value.

6. **Iterative and Agile Processes:** Implement iterative and agile processes that allow for rapid prototyping, testing, and iteration of ideas. Embrace a fail-fast mentality that encourages learning from failures and iterating towards success.

7. **Leadership Support:** Leadership plays a critical role in driving innovation and adaptability. Leaders should demonstrate a commitment to innovation, provide vision and direction, allocate resources, and remove barriers to innovation.

Challenges in Driving Innovation and Adaptability

1. **Risk Aversion:** Organizations may be risk-averse, fearing failure or resistance to change. Overcoming risk aversion requires creating a safe environment for experimentation, learning from failures, and celebrating innovation efforts.

2. **Silos and Communication Barriers:** Silos and communication barriers can hinder collaboration and knowledge sharing. Break down silos through cross-functional teams, open communication channels, and shared goals that promote collaboration and alignment.

3. **Resource Constraints:** Limited resources, budget constraints, and competing priorities can impede innovation efforts. Prioritize innovation investments, leverage external partnerships, and allocate resources strategically to support innovation initiatives.

4. **Resistance to Change:** Employees and stakeholders may resist change due to uncertainty,

fear of disruption, or lack of understanding. Address resistance through communication, stakeholder engagement, and involving employees in the innovation process.

Impact of Driving Innovation and Adaptability

1. **Business Growth and Expansion:** Driving innovation and adaptability leads to business growth by opening new market opportunities, expanding product offerings, and reaching new customer segments.

2. **Market Leadership**: Organizations that drive innovation and adaptability can establish themselves as market leaders, setting trends, and shaping industry standards.

3. **Improved Customer Experience**: Innovation and adaptability enhance the customer experience by delivering innovative products, personalized services, and seamless interactions that meet customer expectations and preferences.

4. **Employee Satisfaction and Retention:** Empowering employees to drive innovation and

adaptability contributes to higher job satisfaction, engagement, and retention. Employees feel valued, challenged, and motivated to contribute their best efforts.

5. **Resilience and Agility:** Innovation and adaptability make organizations more resilient and agile in responding to market changes, disruptions, and uncertainties. They can pivot quickly, iterate on strategies, and capitalize on emerging opportunities.

In conclusion, driving innovation and adaptability is essential for organizations to thrive in today's dynamic and competitive business environment. By fostering a culture of innovation, empowering employees, embracing technology, and overcoming challenges, organizations can unlock new opportunities, drive business growth, and create lasting impact in their industries. Innovation and adaptability are not just strategies but core capabilities that enable organizations to navigate complexity, seize opportunities, and stay ahead of the curve in an ever-evolving marketplace.

CHAPTER 4: LEADING THROUGH CHANGE AND CHALLENGES

Leading through change and challenges is a defining aspect of effective leadership, requiring resilience, adaptability, and strategic vision. In this chapter, we delve into the complexities of leading during times of change, uncertainty, and adversity, exploring strategies, principles, and insights for navigating transitions, overcoming obstacles, and inspiring resilience within teams and organizations.

Change is inevitable in today's fast-paced and dynamic business environment, whether it be technological advancements, market shifts, or internal transformations. Effective leaders understand the importance of leading through change with clarity, empathy, and agility, guiding teams towards success despite challenges and disruptions

Through this chapter, we aim to equip leaders with the knowledge, tools, and perspectives needed to navigate change and challenges effectively. From communication strategies to change management techniques, we explore the multifaceted role of leaders in fostering resilience, driving innovation, and steering organizations towards long-term success in the face of adversity.

Join us on a journey of leadership exploration as we uncover the art of leading through change and challenges, embracing uncertainty as an opportunity for growth, transformation, and organizational resilience. It's time to embrace change, navigate challenges, and inspire greatness as leaders in a rapidly evolving landscape.

- Embracing Change as a Catalyst for Growth

Embracing change as a catalyst for growth is a mindset and strategic approach that organizations and individuals can adopt to leverage opportunities, drive innovation, and achieve long-term success. In this comprehensive discussion, we will explore the importance of embracing change, strategies for doing so effectively, challenges to consider, and the impact it has on organizational growth and development.

Importance of Embracing Change

1. **Adaptability:** Embracing change allows organizations and individuals to adapt quickly to evolving market conditions, technological advancements, and customer preferences. It enables them to stay relevant, competitive, and resilient in a dynamic business environment.

2. **Innovation:** Change often brings opportunities for innovation, creativity, and problem-solving. Embracing change encourages organizations to explore new ideas, experiment with different approaches, and drive continuous improvement and innovation.

3. **Growth Opportunities:** Change can lead to growth opportunities, such as entering new markets,

expanding product lines, or diversifying revenue streams. Embracing change enables organizations to capitalize on these opportunities and unlock their full potential for growth.

4. **Learning and Development:** Change fosters learning and development by challenging individuals and teams to acquire new skills, knowledge, and perspectives. It promotes a culture of continuous learning, adaptation, and personal growth.

Strategies for Embracing Change as a Catalyst for Growth

1. **Cultivate a Growth Mindset:** Encourage a growth mindset among employees, leaders, and stakeholders by promoting a belief in the ability to learn, adapt, and grow from challenges and experiences. Emphasize the value of embracing change as an opportunity for personal and professional development.

2. **Communicate Effectively:** Communicate the rationale, vision, and benefits of change

transparently and consistently. Keep stakeholders informed, engaged, and involved throughout the change process to build understanding, trust, and commitment.

3. **Empower and Support:** Empower employees to embrace change by providing them with the resources, training, and support needed to navigate challenges, acquire new skills, and succeed in a changing environment. Offer coaching, mentorship, and opportunities for growth and development.

4. **Encourage Innovation:** Foster a culture of innovation by encouraging creativity, risk-taking, and experimentation. Provide space for employees to generate and implement innovative ideas that drive growth, efficiency, and customer value.

5. **Collaborate and Share Knowledge:** Foster collaboration, knowledge sharing, and cross-functional teamwork to leverage diverse perspectives, expertise, and experiences. Encourage teams to collaborate on projects, share best

practices, and learn from each other's successes and failures.

6. Anticipate and Prepare: Anticipate and prepare for change by conducting scenario planning, risk assessments, and impact analyses. Develop contingency plans, mitigation strategies, and resilience-building measures to navigate potential challenges and disruptions effectively.

Challenges in Embracing Change

1. **Resistance to Change:** Some individuals and organizations may resist change due to fear of the unknown, loss of control, or perceived risks. Overcoming resistance requires communication, education, and addressing concerns proactively.

2. **Uncertainty and Ambiguity:** Change can bring uncertainty and ambiguity, making it challenging to navigate and plan effectively. Develop clear goals, strategies, and decision-making frameworks to guide actions and minimize uncertainty.

3. **Resource Constraints:** Limited resources, budget constraints, and competing priorities can

hinder efforts to embrace change and drive growth. Prioritize initiatives, allocate resources strategically, and seek opportunities for collaboration and resource-sharing.

4. **Cultural Alignment:** Aligning organizational culture, values, and norms with change initiatives can be challenging. Foster a culture of openness, collaboration, and continuous improvement that supports change and growth efforts.

Impact of Embracing Change as a Catalyst for Growth

1. **Innovation and Agility:** Embracing change fosters innovation, agility, and adaptability within organizations. It enables them to respond quickly to market changes, customer needs, and competitive pressures, driving innovation and competitive advantage.

2. **Organizational Resilience:** Organizations that embrace change are more resilient and able to withstand challenges, disruptions, and uncertainties. They develop the capacity to pivot, iterate, and

reinvent themselves in response to changing circumstances.

3. **Employee Engagement and Retention:** Embracing change positively impacts employee engagement, satisfaction, and retention. Employees feel valued, challenged, and motivated to contribute their skills and ideas to drive organizational growth and success.

4. **Strategic Growth Opportunities:** Embracing change as a catalyst for growth opens up strategic opportunities, such as entering new markets, expanding product lines, or innovating business models. It enables organizations to capitalize on emerging trends and capitalize on market shifts.

5. **Continuous Improvement:** Embracing change promotes a culture of continuous improvement, learning, and adaptation. Organizations continuously evaluate and optimize processes, products, and services to enhance quality, efficiency, and customer value.

In conclusion, embracing change as a catalyst for growth is essential for organizations seeking to thrive in a rapidly evolving business landscape. By cultivating a growth mindset, communicating effectively, empowering employees, fostering innovation, and addressing challenges proactively, organizations can leverage change as an opportunity for growth, innovation, and long-term success. Embracing change not only drives organizational growth but also fosters a culture of resilience, agility, and continuous improvement that enables organizations to navigate challenges and seize opportunities in an ever-changing world.

- Resilience in the Face of Adversity

Resilience in the face of adversity is a critical skill and mindset that enables individuals and organizations to navigate challenges, setbacks, and hardships effectively. It involves the ability to bounce back from adversity, adapt to change, and thrive in the face of uncertainty. In this comprehensive discussion, we will explore the importance of resilience, strategies for building resilience, challenges to consider, and the impact it has on personal and organizational well-being.

Importance of Resilience

1. **Adaptability:** Resilience enables individuals and organizations to adapt quickly to changing circumstances, unexpected events, and external pressures. It fosters flexibility, agility, and the ability to pivot in response to challenges.

2. **Emotional Well-being:** Resilience contributes to emotional well-being by helping individuals cope with stress, manage emotions, and maintain a positive outlook in challenging situations. It promotes self-awareness, self-regulation, and emotional intelligence.

3. **Problem-Solving:** Resilient individuals are effective problem solvers who approach challenges with a solution-oriented mindset. They identify

opportunities, learn from failures, and develop creative strategies to overcome obstacles.

4. **Persistence:** Resilience fuels persistence and perseverance in pursuing goals and aspirations. It helps individuals stay motivated, focused, and determined to achieve success despite setbacks and setbacks.

Strategies for Building Resilience

1. **Cultivate a Growth Mindset:** Adopt a growth mindset that views challenges as opportunities for learning and growth. Embrace failures as learning experiences, focus on continuous improvement, and believe in your ability to overcome obstacles.

2. **Develop Coping Skills:** Develop coping skills and strategies to manage stress, anxiety, and adversity effectively. Practice mindfulness, relaxation techniques, and positive self-talk to build resilience and enhance well-being.

3. **Build a Support Network:** Build a strong support network of family, friends, colleagues, and mentors who can provide emotional support,

encouragement, and guidance during tough times. Seek help when needed and connect with others who share similar experiences.

4. Set Realistic Goals: Set realistic goals, priorities, and expectations that align with your values, strengths, and resources. Break goals into manageable steps, celebrate progress, and stay focused on long-term objectives.

5. **Adaptability and Flexibility:** Develop adaptability and flexibility in responding to change and uncertainty. Be open to new ideas, perspectives, and opportunities. Embrace change as a chance for growth and innovation.

6. **Practice Self-Care:** Prioritize self-care activities that promote physical, mental, and emotional well-being. Get enough sleep, exercise regularly, eat healthily, and engage in activities that bring joy and fulfillment.

Challenges in Building Resilience

1. **Fear of Failure:** Fear of failure can hinder resilience by causing individuals to avoid risks,

challenges, and new opportunities. Overcome fear of failure by reframing setbacks as learning experiences and focusing on growth and improvement.

2. **Perfectionism:** Perfectionism can lead to excessive self-criticism, stress, and burnout, undermining resilience. Practice self-compassion, accept imperfections, and celebrate progress rather than striving for perfection.

3. **Isolation:** Isolation and lack of social support can weaken resilience. Build and nurture meaningful connections with others, seek social support, and engage in activities that foster a sense of belonging and connection.

4. **Overwhelm:** Feeling overwhelmed by challenges, responsibilities, and expectations can deplete resilience. Prioritize tasks, set boundaries, and practice time management to avoid burnout and maintain balance.

Impact of Resilience

1. **Improved Coping Skills:** Resilience enhances coping skills, emotional regulation, and stress management. Individuals can navigate challenges, setbacks, and crises with composure, adaptability, and confidence.

2. **Enhanced Problem-Solving:** Resilient individuals are effective problem solvers who approach challenges with creativity, optimism, and determination. They identify solutions, learn from failures, and persevere in achieving goals.

3. **Positive Outlook:** Resilience fosters a positive outlook, optimism, and hopefulness even in difficult times. Individuals can maintain perspective, focus on strengths, and find meaning and purpose in adversity.

4. **Healthy Relationships:** Resilience strengthens relationships by promoting empathy, communication, and support. Individuals can connect with others authentically, build trust, and navigate conflicts constructively.

5. **Personal Growth:** Resilience fuels personal growth, self-discovery, and self-improvement. Individuals can learn from challenges, develop new skills, and become more adaptable, resilient, and resourceful.

In conclusion, resilience in the face of adversity is a valuable asset that individuals and organizations can cultivate to thrive in challenging times. By adopting strategies such as developing a growth mindset, building coping skills, nurturing social connections, and practicing self-care, individuals can strengthen their resilience and navigate challenges effectively. Resilience not only enhances personal well-being but also fosters a culture of adaptability, innovation, and collaboration within organizations, leading to greater success and resilience as a collective.

- Strategies for Managing Conflict Effectively

Managing conflict effectively is crucial for maintaining positive relationships, fostering collaboration, and achieving productive outcomes. In this comprehensive discussion, we will explore the importance of conflict management, strategies for managing conflict effectively, challenges to consider, and the impact it has on relationships and organizational success.

Importance of Conflict Management

1. **Improved Communication:** Effective conflict management promotes open communication, transparency, and understanding among individuals and teams. It encourages dialogue, active listening, and the exchange of ideas and perspectives.

2. **Resolution of Issues:** Conflict management facilitates the resolution of issues, disagreements, and disputes in a constructive manner. It helps identify underlying causes, explore solutions, and reach agreements that meet the needs of all parties involved.

3. **Relationship Building:** Managing conflict effectively strengthens relationships by building trust, respect, and empathy. It fosters collaboration,

teamwork, and a sense of unity among individuals and teams.

4. Enhanced Problem-Solving: Conflict management enhances problem-solving skills by encouraging critical thinking, creativity, and cooperation. It enables individuals to identify root causes, brainstorm solutions, and implement effective strategies to address challenges.

Strategies for Managing Conflict Effectively

1. **Promote Open Communication:** Encourage open and honest communication to address issues, concerns, and misunderstandings proactively. Create a safe space for individuals to express their thoughts, feelings, and perspectives without fear of judgment or reprisal.

2. **Active Listening:** Practice active listening by paying attention, empathizing, and seeking to understand others' viewpoints. Listen without interrupting, clarify understanding, and reflect back what you hear to demonstrate empathy and validation.

3. **Clarify Expectations:** Clarify expectations, roles, and responsibilities to avoid misunderstandings and conflicts. Establish clear guidelines, policies, and procedures for decision-making, communication channels, and conflict resolution processes.

4. **Seek Common Ground:** Focus on finding common ground and shared interests to bridge differences and build consensus. Look for win-win solutions that address everyone's needs and concerns while fostering cooperation and collaboration.

5. **Use Collaborative Problem-Solving:** Engage in collaborative problem-solving approaches, such as brainstorming, mediation, or negotiation, to find mutually beneficial solutions. Involve all parties in the decision-making process and seek input from diverse perspectives.

6. **Manage Emotions:** Manage emotions effectively during conflict by staying calm, composed, and respectful. Avoid reacting impulsively or

emotionally, and focus on addressing issues objectively and constructively.

7. **Set Boundaries:** Establish clear boundaries and ground rules for behavior, communication, and conflict resolution. Define acceptable conduct, conflict escalation procedures, and consequences for violating established boundaries.

8. **Encourage Feedback:** Encourage feedback, constructive criticism, and alternative viewpoints as opportunities for learning and growth. Create a culture that values feedback, encourages dialogue, and promotes continuous improvement.

Challenges in Managing Conflict Effectively

1. **Emotional Intensity:** Conflicts can involve strong emotions, such as anger, frustration, or hurt feelings, which may escalate tensions and hinder resolution efforts. Manage emotional intensity by staying calm, empathetic, and focused on problem-solving.

2. **Differing Perspectives:** Conflicts often arise from differing perspectives, values, and priorities

among individuals or groups. Bridge differences by seeking common ground, understanding diverse viewpoints, and promoting empathy and respect.

3. **Power Imbalance:** Power imbalances can affect conflict dynamics, with individuals or groups feeling disadvantaged or marginalized. Address power dynamics by promoting fairness, transparency, and inclusivity in decision-making and conflict resolution processes.

4. **Communication Barriers:** Communication barriers, such as language differences, misinterpretations, or ineffective communication styles, can hinder conflict resolution efforts. Overcome barriers by using clear, concise language, active listening techniques, and seeking clarification when needed.

Impact of Effective Conflict Management

1. **Improved Relationships:** Effective conflict management strengthens relationships by building trust, understanding, and respect among individuals

and teams. It fosters a positive work environment, collaboration, and mutual support.

2. **Enhanced Problem-Solving:** Conflict management enhances problem-solving skills and decision-making by encouraging critical thinking, creativity, and collaboration. It enables individuals and teams to address challenges effectively and implement solutions that meet organizational goals.

3. **Increased Productivity:** Resolving conflicts promptly and effectively minimizes disruptions, distractions, and negative impacts on productivity. It enables individuals and teams to stay focused, engaged, and motivated to achieve goals and objectives.

4. **Positive Organizational Culture:** Effective conflict management contributes to a positive organizational culture that values open communication, collaboration, and continuous improvement. It promotes a culture of accountability, transparency, and resilience.

5. **Conflict Prevention:** Effective conflict management strategies can also prevent conflicts from escalating or recurring in the future. By addressing underlying issues, promoting understanding, and fostering proactive communication, organizations can create a more harmonious and productive work environment.

In conclusion, effective conflict management is essential for promoting positive relationships, fostering collaboration, and achieving organizational success. By promoting open communication, active listening, collaborative problem-solving, and managing emotions effectively, individuals and organizations can navigate conflicts constructively and turn challenges into opportunities for growth and learning. Effective conflict management not only resolves conflicts but also strengthens relationships, enhances problem-solving skills, and contributes to a positive organizational culture built on trust, respect, and collaboration.

CHAPTER 5: LEAVING A LASTING LEADERSHIP LEGACY

Leaving a lasting leadership legacy is the culmination of a leader's journey—a testament to their impact, influence, and contributions to individuals, teams, and organizations. In this chapter, we explore the essence of leadership legacy, the importance of legacy-building, strategies for creating a lasting impact, and the significance of succession planning.

A leader's legacy extends beyond their tenure, shaping organizational culture, values, and practices for years to come. It encompasses the imprint they leave on people's lives, the legacy of accomplishments and milestones achieved, and the enduring principles and beliefs that guide future generations of leaders.

Join us as we delve into the elements that define a meaningful leadership legacy, from vision and values to mentorship and succession planning. Discover how leaders can leave a lasting impact, inspire others, and create a legacy that continues to inspire and guide long after they have moved on.

Through insightful discussions, real-world examples, and practical guidance, we aim to inspire leaders to reflect on their legacy, identify opportunities for impact, and cultivate a legacy mindset that shapes a positive and enduring legacy for themselves and their organizations. It's time to explore the legacy you want to leave and the steps to make it a reality.

- Defining Your Leadership Legacy Vision

Defining your leadership legacy vision is a strategic process that involves clarifying your values, goals, and desired impact as a leader. It encompasses the legacy you aspire to leave behind, the contributions you want to make, and the lasting impact you aim to create within your organization, community, or industry. In this comprehensive discussion, we will explore the importance of defining your leadership legacy vision, strategies for doing so effectively, challenges to consider, and the impact it has on your leadership journey and legacy.

Importance of Defining Your Leadership Legacy Vision

1. **Alignment with Values:** Defining your leadership legacy vision aligns your actions and decisions with your core values, beliefs, and principles. It provides a guiding framework for leading authentically and staying true to your values in challenging situations.

2. **Clarity of Purpose:** A clear leadership legacy vision provides clarity of purpose and direction, helping you set meaningful goals, priorities, and

strategies. It serves as a compass that guides your leadership journey and decision-making processes.

3. **Inspiration and Motivation:** Your leadership legacy vision inspires and motivates you to strive for excellence, pursue ambitious goals, and make a positive impact. It fuels your passion, resilience, and commitment to achieving long-term success and leaving a lasting legacy.

4. **Guidance for Decision-Making:** Your leadership legacy vision serves as a guidepost for making strategic decisions, prioritizing initiatives, and allocating resources. It helps you evaluate opportunities, risks, and trade-offs in alignment with your long-term vision and goals.

Strategies for Defining Your Leadership Legacy Vision

1. **Reflect on Values and Beliefs:** Begin by reflecting on your core values, beliefs, and principles that define who you are as a leader. Identify what matters most to you, what inspires you, and what legacy you want to leave behind.

2. **Clarify Goals and Impact:** Define specific goals and outcomes you want to achieve as part of your leadership legacy. Consider the impact you want to have on individuals, teams, organizations, and stakeholders. Be specific about the changes, improvements, or transformations you envision.

3. **Engage Stakeholders:** Engage with stakeholders, including team members, peers, mentors, and stakeholders, to gather feedback, insights, and perspectives. Seek input on your leadership legacy vision, values, and goals to ensure alignment and buy-in.

4. **Create a Vision Statement:** Develop a clear and concise vision statement that articulates your leadership legacy vision, values, goals, and desired impact. Your vision statement should inspire, resonate, and provide a compelling direction for your leadership journey.

5. **Set Measurable Objectives:** Translate your leadership legacy vision into actionable and measurable objectives. Define key performance

indicators (KPIs), milestones, and success criteria to track progress and evaluate the impact of your leadership efforts.

6. **Develop a Strategic Plan:** Develop a strategic plan that outlines the strategies, initiatives, and actions required to achieve your leadership legacy vision. Define roles, responsibilities, timelines, and resources needed to execute your plan effectively.

Challenges in Defining Your Leadership Legacy Vision

1. **Uncertainty and Ambiguity:** Defining your leadership legacy vision may involve uncertainty and ambiguity, especially in complex and rapidly changing environments. Embrace ambiguity as an opportunity for exploration, learning, and adaptation.

2. **Alignment with Organizational Culture:** Ensure that your leadership legacy vision aligns with the values, mission, and culture of your organization. Navigate potential conflicts or discrepancies by finding common ground and

fostering alignment with organizational goals and priorities.

3. **Resistance to Change:** Some stakeholders may resist changes or initiatives associated with your leadership legacy vision. Address resistance through communication, engagement, and addressing concerns or misconceptions proactively.

4. **Managing Expectations:** Manage expectations and avoid overcommitting or setting unrealistic goals as part of your leadership legacy vision. Set achievable milestones, communicate progress transparently, and adjust plans as needed based on feedback and results.

Impact of Defining Your Leadership Legacy Vision

1. **Inspired Leadership:** Defining your leadership legacy vision inspires you to lead with purpose, passion, and authenticity. It fuels your motivation, resilience, and commitment to making a positive difference in the lives of others.

2. **Strategic Alignment:** Your leadership legacy vision fosters strategic alignment within your organization, team, or community. It ensures that everyone is working towards common goals, values, and outcomes, driving unity and collaboration.

3. **Accountability and Evaluation:** Your leadership legacy vision provides a basis for accountability and evaluation of your leadership effectiveness. It enables you to track progress, measure impact, and adjust strategies to achieve desired outcomes.

4. **Long-Term Impact:** By defining your leadership legacy vision, you create a roadmap for long-term impact and sustainability. Your vision guides your actions, decisions, and investments in initiatives that contribute to your legacy and enduring positive change.

In conclusion, defining your leadership legacy vision is a transformative process that shapes your leadership journey, impact, and legacy. By aligning with your values, clarifying goals, engaging stakeholders, and developing a strategic plan, you can create a compelling vision that inspires, guides, and drives meaningful change. Your leadership legacy vision serves as a legacy-building blueprint that leaves a lasting impact on individuals, organizations, and communities, reflecting your values, contributions, and aspirations as a leader.

- Mentoring and Developing Future Leaders

Mentoring and developing future leaders is a strategic and impactful process that involves guiding, nurturing, and empowering individuals to reach their full potential and assume leadership roles. In this comprehensive discussion, we will explore the importance of mentoring and developing future leaders, strategies for effective mentorship, challenges to consider, and the impact it has on organizational success and succession planning.

Importance of Mentoring and Developing Future Leaders

1. **Succession Planning:** Mentoring and developing future leaders are critical components of succession planning. By identifying and grooming high-potential individuals, organizations can ensure a smooth transition of leadership roles and continuity of strategic vision.

2. **Leadership Pipeline:** Mentoring and developing future leaders contribute to building a robust leadership pipeline within organizations. It ensures a steady supply of qualified and capable leaders who can step into key positions and drive organizational growth and success.

3. **Knowledge Transfer:** Mentoring allows experienced leaders to share their knowledge, insights, and expertise with emerging leaders. It facilitates knowledge transfer, skill development, and the cultivation of leadership capabilities

necessary for navigating complex challenges and opportunities.

4. **Engagement and Retention:** Mentoring programs contribute to employee engagement, satisfaction, and retention by providing opportunities for learning, growth, and professional development. They demonstrate organizational investment in employees' career advancement and well-being.

Strategies for Mentoring and Developing Future Leaders

1. **Identify High-Potential Talent:** Begin by identifying high-potential individuals within your organization who demonstrate leadership potential, initiative, and a growth mindset. Consider performance evaluations, feedback from supervisors, and assessments of skills and competencies.

2. **Establish Mentorship Programs:** Implement formal mentorship programs that pair experienced leaders with emerging talent. Match mentors and

mentees based on skills, goals, interests, and compatibility to facilitate meaningful and productive mentoring relationships.

3. **Set Clear Objectives and Expectations:** Define clear objectives, goals, and expectations for mentoring relationships. Establish a framework for regular meetings, communication channels, and developmental activities that support mentees' growth and progress.

4. **Provide Learning Opportunities:** Offer learning opportunities, training programs, workshops, and resources that support mentees' development as future leaders. Focus on areas such as leadership skills, communication, decision-making, strategic thinking, and emotional intelligence.

5. **Encourage Feedback and Reflection:** Encourage open and honest feedback between mentors and mentees to facilitate learning, growth, and self-awareness. Create a safe and supportive

environment for reflection, self-assessment, and goal setting.

6. **Promote Networking and Exposure:** Facilitate networking opportunities, job rotations, cross-functional projects, and exposure to senior leadership roles for mentees. Encourage mentees to broaden their perspectives, build relationships, and gain diverse experiences.

7. **Support Career Planning:** Support mentees in developing personalized career development plans that align with their strengths, interests, and aspirations. Provide guidance, coaching, and resources to help them navigate career paths, set goals, and achieve milestones.

Challenges in Mentoring and Developing Future Leaders

1. **Time Constraints:** Busy schedules and competing priorities may pose challenges for mentors and mentees to dedicate sufficient time and attention to mentoring relationships. Establish clear

expectations, scheduling guidelines, and support systems to overcome time constraints.

2. **Skill and Knowledge Gaps:** Mentors and mentees may encounter skill and knowledge gaps that require additional support, training, or resources. Provide access to learning opportunities, subject matter experts, and developmental resources to address gaps effectively.

3. **Communication Barriers:** Communication barriers, such as misalignment of expectations, ineffective feedback, or lack of clarity, can hinder effective mentoring relationships. Foster open communication, active listening, and regular check-ins to overcome communication barriers.

4. **Resistance to Change:** Some individuals may resist mentorship or developmental initiatives due to fear of change, reluctance to seek feedback, or lack of awareness of the benefits. Communicate the value of mentorship, address concerns, and highlight success stories to promote engagement and participation.

Impact of Mentoring and Developing Future Leaders

1. **Leadership Development:** Mentoring and developing future leaders contribute to the development of a talent pipeline with strong leadership capabilities, strategic thinking, and decision-making skills. It prepares individuals to assume leadership roles with confidence and competence.

2. **Succession Readiness:** Effective mentoring programs enhance succession readiness by grooming successors, filling leadership gaps, and ensuring a smooth transition of key roles. They mitigate risks associated with leadership turnover and changes in organizational leadership.

3. **Employee Engagement and Retention:** Mentoring programs boost employee engagement, satisfaction, and retention by providing opportunities for career growth, skill development, and professional support. They foster a culture of

learning, development, and investment in employees' long-term success.

4. **Organizational Performance:** Mentoring and developing future leaders contribute to organizational performance, innovation, and competitiveness. They cultivate a diverse talent pool, foster leadership diversity, and drive business results through effective leadership and talent management.

In conclusion, mentoring and developing future leaders are essential strategies for building a strong leadership pipeline, driving organizational success, and ensuring continuity of leadership excellence. By investing in mentorship programs, identifying high-potential talent, providing learning opportunities, and addressing challenges proactively, organizations can develop a culture of leadership development and talent growth. Mentoring future leaders not only prepares individuals for leadership roles but also contributes to employee engagement, retention, and organizational resilience in an ever-evolving business landscape.

- Sustaining a Legacy of Impact and Influence

Sustaining a legacy of impact and influence is a strategic endeavor that involves maintaining and building upon the positive contributions, reputation, and influence established over time. It requires continuous effort, adaptation, and alignment with core values and goals. In this comprehensive discussion, we will explore the importance of sustaining a legacy, strategies for doing so effectively, challenges to consider, and the impact it has on individuals, organizations, and communities.

Importance of Sustaining a Legacy of Impact and Influence

1. **Continuity of Impact:** Sustaining a legacy ensures that the positive impact, initiatives, and contributions made by individuals or organizations continue to benefit stakeholders, communities, and

society. It preserves the momentum of progress and maintains a focus on long-term goals and outcomes.

2. **Reputation and Credibility:** A sustained legacy of impact and influence enhances reputation, credibility, and trust among stakeholders, including customers, partners, investors, and the public. It reinforces the values, integrity, and commitment to excellence that define the legacy.

3. **Inspiration and Motivation:** A sustained legacy serves as an inspiration and source of motivation for current and future generations. It demonstrates what is possible through vision, dedication, and perseverance, inspiring others to strive for excellence and make a difference.

4. **Continued Growth and Innovation:** Sustaining a legacy fosters a culture of continuous growth, innovation, and improvement. It encourages individuals and organizations to adapt to changing circumstances, embrace new opportunities, and evolve while staying true to core values and principles.

Strategies for Sustaining a Legacy of Impact and Influence

1. **Align with Core Values:** Ensure that initiatives, decisions, and actions align with the core values, mission, and purpose that define the legacy. Maintain a strong commitment to ethical conduct, social responsibility, and integrity in all endeavors.

2. **Adapt to Change:** Embrace change and innovation while staying true to foundational principles. Continuously assess market trends, stakeholder needs, and external factors to adapt strategies, approaches, and solutions as needed.

3. **Empower Successors:** Empower and mentor successors to carry forward the legacy and build upon past achievements. Provide guidance, support, and opportunities for leadership development to ensure a smooth transition and continuity of impact.

4. **Collaborate and Partner:** Collaborate with like-minded individuals, organizations, and stakeholders to amplify impact, leverage resources, and address

complex challenges collectively. Build strategic partnerships that enhance capabilities, expand reach, and drive meaningful change.

5. **Communicate Effectively:** Communicate the legacy's vision, impact, and accomplishments effectively to stakeholders, the public, and future generations. Share success stories, lessons learned, and best practices to inspire, educate, and mobilize support.

6. **Measure and Evaluate Impact:** Use data, metrics, and feedback mechanisms to measure and evaluate the impact of initiatives and activities associated with the legacy. Identify areas of strength, areas for improvement, and opportunities for further impact.

Challenges in Sustaining a Legacy of Impact and Influence

1. **Maintaining Relevance:** Sustaining a legacy requires staying relevant in a dynamic and competitive environment. Address challenges such as technological advancements, market changes,

and shifting stakeholder expectations by adapting strategies and embracing innovation.

2. **Succession Planning:** Ensuring a smooth transition of leadership and stewardship is crucial for sustaining a legacy. Develop and implement succession plans, mentorship programs, and leadership development initiatives to groom successors and preserve continuity.

3. **Managing Change:** Managing change within the organization or community while maintaining the legacy's core values and principles can be challenging. Foster open communication, engagement, and collaboration to navigate change effectively and build consensus around strategic directions.

4. **Resource Allocation:** Balancing resource allocation between sustaining current initiatives and investing in future growth and innovation requires careful planning and prioritization. Optimize resource utilization, explore diverse funding

sources, and leverage partnerships to maximize impact.

Impact of Sustaining a Legacy of Impact and Influence

1. **Long-Term Sustainability:** Sustaining a legacy ensures long-term sustainability and resilience of initiatives, programs, and projects. It fosters a culture of responsible stewardship, continuous improvement, and adaptive leadership.

2. **Inspiration and Leadership:** A sustained legacy of impact and influence inspires others to take action, lead by example, and make meaningful contributions to society. It sets a standard of excellence, leadership, and social responsibility that motivates individuals and organizations to excel.

3. **Community and Stakeholder Trust:** Sustaining a legacy builds trust, credibility, and goodwill among communities, stakeholders, and partners. It fosters strong relationships, collaboration, and support networks that enhance collective impact and sustainability.

4. **Innovation and Adaptation:** A sustained legacy encourages innovation, creativity, and adaptation to changing needs and challenges. It promotes a culture of continuous learning, experimentation, and agility that drives progress and resilience over time.

In conclusion, sustaining a legacy of impact and influence requires strategic vision, commitment to core values, collaboration, and adaptability. By aligning initiatives with core values, empowering successors, fostering collaboration, and effectively communicating impact, individuals and organizations can sustain their legacy and continue making a positive difference in the world. A sustained legacy inspires others, fosters innovation, builds trust, and contributes to long-term sustainability, resilience, and success.

CONCLUSION

In "Leadership Legacy: Nurturing Authentic Influence and Impactful Management," we have embarked on a transformative journey exploring the essence of leadership legacy, the power of authentic influence, and the significance of impactful management. Through insightful discussions, real-world examples, and practical guidance, we have delved into the core principles and strategies that define a meaningful leadership legacy and drive positive change in individuals, organizations, and communities.

As we conclude this journey, it is clear that nurturing authentic influence and impactful management are not just aspirations but essential pillars of effective leadership. We have learned that leadership is not merely about titles or positions but about the profound impact we have on others, the legacy we leave behind, and the enduring influence that shapes the future.

Our exploration has underscored the importance of aligning leadership actions with core values, fostering trust and transparency, embracing diversity and inclusion, and empowering others to reach their full potential. We have explored the role of mentorship, collaboration, and continuous learning in shaping future leaders and sustaining a legacy of positive impact and influence.

As leaders, we are entrusted with a profound responsibility—to inspire, guide, and empower those around us; to lead with integrity, empathy, and resilience; and to leave a lasting legacy that transcends our time. It is through our collective efforts, shared values, and commitment to excellence that we can nurture authentic influence, cultivate impactful management practices, and shape a brighter future for generations to come.

May this book serve as a roadmap for leaders aspiring to make a difference, build meaningful legacies, and leave an indelible mark on the world. Let us continue to lead with purpose, passion, and authenticity, knowing that our legacy is not just what we achieve but the lives we touch, the values we uphold, and the positive change we inspire.

Thank you for joining me on this enriching journey of exploring leadership legacy, nurturing authentic influence, and embracing impactful management. Together, let us continue to strive for excellence, make a difference, and leave a lasting legacy of positive impact and influence in our organizations and beyond.

www.ingramcontent.com/pod-product-compliance
Lightning Source LLC
Chambersburg PA
CBHW070151230526
45471CB00002B/609